ISBN-13: 978-1979784399
ISBN- 10: 1979782396

Me and My #HigherSelf

A Book of Memes to Channel Your Inner Wisdom

Bunny Michael

for Khara

who's love continually
helps me find my
Higher Self

Me: How do
I love myself?

Higher Self:
Stop trying
to convince
yourself that
you don't.

Me: I'm afraid of failing.

Higher Self: What if I told you that you were actually afraid of succeeding cus then you would have to accept your power- something you have been resisting for far too long.

Me: I am right
and you are
wrong.

Higher Self:
I am willing to
see your
perspective
so you can
see mine.

9

Me: I'll never be successful... people don't really like me... I wish I was more fit... what if I never make money...

Higher Self: You are literally addicted to being mean to yourself and I am cutting you off.

**Me: I'm so sensitive.
I really hate it.**

**Higher Self: Sensitivity
is intuitive wisdom that
has been suppressed
for generations leading
us not to trust our
hearts,
which is a big
reason the planet is so
off balanced. You are
actually incredibly
wise.**

Me: I will be
happy when
that person
changes.

Higher Self: I
will be happy
when I change
my mind about
what I need from
that person. 12

Me: There is so much war and conflict in the world, how can anything change?

Higher Self: Our outer world is a reflection of our inner world. We are at war with ourselves and other people in our minds everyday. Change is possible in the world because it's possible in you. 14

Me:
Life's hard.

Higher Self:
So maybe you should stop being so hard on yourself.

Me: Everyone I talk to is going through some really hard times. All their issues are coming up.

Higher Self: We are experiencing a massive evolutionary awakening, and just like a wound in the body, the puss has to surface for the real healing to begin.

Me: I'm a bipolar addict with childhood trauma and high anxiety.

Higher Self: I was born into a world of insanity and numbed myself for survival. I deeply feel the pain of humanity and have the strength to heal it.

Me: Its so hard to put yourself out there, ya know, make art and stuff, people are so judgmental.

Higher Self: So you're just gonna sit around and judge the "judgemental" people to keep from being judged meanwhile you're sitting here still judging yourself? Hmmmmm...

19

Me: I'm worried.

**Higher Self:
Your mind is so
powerful that when
you worry about
something you're
feeling all the effects
of it actually happening.
You're manifesting
that reality and your
body feels the stress
your mind creates.
Worrying is another
form of self sabotage
because you're creating
your own suffering.**

Me: Sometimes I have these glimpses of happiness but holding on to them feels difficult.

Higher Self: It feels difficult because it's different. Happiness can feel scary when you're so used to feeling bad.

Me: I really love this
person but I'm afraid
of being hurt.

Higher Self: Sweetie,
you've experienced
trauma and abuse
before so being
afraid of being
hurt makes sense.
But this is now, it's not
your past. You deserve
love. You are so strong.
Let yourself receive it.

Me: F*ck
the haters.

Higher Self:
Love the
haters cus
love is a
transformational
frequency that
obliterates the
illusion that
hatred has power.

Me: I wanna to go out tonight but my social anxiety is really bad. What's wrong with me?

Higher Self: There is not one person who doesn't experience social anxiety on some level. Go out or stay home but you're not gonna spend the night beating yourself up.

Me: Why do I have so many negative thoughts?

Higher Self: Negative thinking can be a powerful addiction. Like any other addictions, you identify it with who you are. But you are not your thoughts, you are the awareness behind them and you can choose to think differently.

Me: I need a safe space.

Higher Self: I'm right here.

Me: I want to be
popular.
I want more fans,
more likes,
more success.
I know that will make
me happy.

Higher Self: When
happiness depends
on getting more,
no amount will ever
be enough.

Me: I can't figure out what I'm supposed to be doing with my life.

Higher Self: Life isn't something to figure out. It's not a problem to be solved. It's a journey of growing into your highest potential. Your highest potential is being the loving and compassionate person you were created to be. Make that what you're "supposed to be doing" and watch everything fall into place.

Me: We are living
in a post-truth era.

Higher Self: We are
living in a time
when our
deepest truths
are being revealed.

Me: Why does God allow horrible things to happen in the world?

Higher Self: Why do we?

Me: Things are rough out there, I just wanna check out.

Higher Self: Things are rough out there, time to check in.

Me: What that person did to me was so rude. What an assh*le.

Higher Self: I can see that person's inability to be kind is a result of their wounds that need healing and through the strength of compassion their actions don't have the power to hurt my spirit.

Me: I have a right to be angry!

Higher Self: Yes you do and anger has its place in your process but remember there's a point where it stops serving you. There's a point where if you don't let it go it will take you down.

Me: I want my life to come together perfectly.

Higher Self: Life comes together when you let go of your need for perfection.

Me: Everything is so uncertain.

Higher Self: That's a beautiful place for things to be because all possibilities are open and you can create something spectacular.

Me: I know its wrong
but I keep comparing
myself to other people.

Higher Self: Is any
flower better than
another flower?
Is any animal
more important
than another?
We are Nature,
part of a whole,
born with unique
gifts. There is no
comparison.

Me: You tell me to "let go of the past" but how? It's not like I can forget what has happened to me.

Higher Self: Letting go means releasing your attachment. We use our past like a security blanket sometimes and that's why we make the same mistakes and recreate present situations that mirror our past trauma.

Me: I'm afraid of the future.

Higher Self: The future doesn't exist- only the present moment does. So really you are afraid in this moment and you don't have to be. In fact, you're addicted to being afraid. And I don't want you to have to live like this anymore.

41

Me: I don't fit in anywhere.

Higher Self: That's because you're expansive beyond measure.

Me: I feel so out of place in this world.

Higher Self: In a world whose status quo commits war in the name of peace, calls trans children predators, makes you an extremist for saying a black person's life matters, throws away 1/3 of their food supply while 1/9 of the population starves- if you don't feel out of place in this world you would be dead asleep.

Me: I want to succeed but I dunno if I have what it takes.

Higher Self: Humanity shares the same "success" which is awakening to our greatest creative potential and using that magic to bring about love and equality on the planet. So "what it takes" is your decision to step up to the role you are greatly needed for.

Me: I really don't like that person. Remember last time I saw them they were so negative. Its like "chill, learn to let things go!"

Higher Self: That happened 2 months ago. When are you gonna let it go?

46

Me: The times I've been sexually assaulted still haunt me. I still struggle today. But I also feel really strong too cus I got through that.

Higher Self: Our greatest challenges give us our deepest wisdom.

Me: When I'm feeling depressed I just wanna numb it with a weed or a drink or a pill.

Higher Self: That's totally understandable. Remember tho that just like physical pain, emotional pain can be a sign of a part of you that needs healing. When you numb you cover up the symptoms but miss seeing the core of the issue.

Me: I'm haunted by my painful past.

Higher Self:
Your experiences taught you how strong you are and gave you insight to help people who are experiencing the same pain. When you realize the wisdom you have to give the past is not your prison, it is your salvation and part of the salvation of the world.

**Me: Why are people
so evil?**

**Higher Self: There is a
force in this world who's
goal is to kill the human
spirit. This force
has seduced people with
false promises. Its taken
hold of people's deepest
fears of being unlovable.
But what we can't forget is
that our spirit is Eternal, it's
within us all and it is the
Power that will destroy the
evil in this world.**

Me: I have to
love myself
first before
I can love you.

Higher Self:
I am love and
so are you.

Me: I wanna be
famous.

Higher Self:
I want to connect
with as many
people as I can
so we can heal
each other
through
our shared
experience.

53

Me: What do you do when you love someone but you know the relationship is unhealthy? I feel lost in all the fighting and I can't keep going this way.

Higher Self: Love has healthy boundaries. Love says no alot. Enabling this behavior not only hurts you but hurts them too. Sometimes really loving someone is letting them go.

Me:
I'm lonely.

Higher Self:
I'm learning to enjoy solitude.

Me: If this circumstance changed then I would be peaceful.

Higher Self: When I connect to the peace within myself I will see the circumstances differently.

Me: I hope when I die I go to heaven.

Higher Self: What if I told you heaven is a dimensional shift in frequency to a state of loving awareness you can experience right now in this moment.

Me: Ignorance is bliss.

Higher Self: Becoming fully aware then transcending the bullshit through an elevated state of consciousness and using that wisdom to be the change you wanna see in the world is bliss.

Me: Coming out at 15 was hard cus my family didn't accept me.

Higher Self: What you couldn't have known then is that you were teaching your family a great wisdom about our nature and humanity. And they should be grateful for that.

Me: Sometimes I feel ashamed of myself.

Higher Self: Don't be ashamed of not always getting it right. Don't be ashamed of how you feel. Don't be ashamed of where you come from. Don't be ashamed of who you are. You are infinite light dwelling in human form blooming with the creative power of the Universe. Don't ever be ashamed of that.

Me: I've got my successes and I've got my failures.

Higher Self: Failure becomes success when you learn from it.

62

Me: What does
the world
have to offer
me?

Higher Self:
What can I
offer the
world?

63

65

Me: How can I forgive that person? What they did was wrong.

Higher Self: What if I told you forgiveness is not condoning behavior, but letting go of its power to affect your inner peace.

Me: I'm looking
for love.

Higher Self:
I'm looking
to tear down
any walls
I have from
letting love in.

Me: I've been abused in the past so I put up a lot of walls.

Higher Self: Those walls were necessary at a time when you had to protect yourself. The beautiful thing is now you don't need them cus that experience showed you how strong you are. Now you can let them go.

Me: I wish I could know the future.

Higher Self: Then you'd have no say in creating it.

Me: I want to be
recognized by
other people for
my art.

Higher Self:
My art is
to recognize
myself in other
people.

Me: I'm afraid to call people out, especially on controversial issues cus I don't wanna cause problems. I don't wanna hurt anyone's feelings, sometimes my own friends and family.

Higher Self: Love knows how to say what must be said. Love is courage. Love knows people must learn. Love uplifts people out of the bounds of their own misguided actions. Have faith in your voice, speak from your heart, because staying silent doesn't serve them or you.

Me: I can't get over the past.

Higher Self:
I rise above
the past when
I see all my
experiences
as the
curriculum
for self growth.

Me: I'm afraid
of change.

Higher Self:
Change is
inevitable. Your
resistance to
it is creating
an unnatural
anxiety because
it's your
nature to grow.

Me: Ugh why do I feel so moody today?

Higher Self: Cus you're a beautiful sensitive intelligent being who is attuned to the changing energies of your environment. Take a deep breath and accept your feelings because they are totally ok.

Me: Why does PMS make me feel crazy?

Higher Self:
You have been taught that intuitive magic and feeling the pain of the world isn't your inner feminine genius healing power- it's you being "crazy" "over-emotional" or "too sensitive".
Boo, you're a queen and queens feel deep.

Me: Why do I get jealous of other people's success?

Higher Self: Success is an energy- it's an opening to abundance all around you. When you reject it in others it's because deep down you think you don't deserve it either. Every person is a mirror to how we feel about ourselves.

Me: I want to be right.

Higher Self: I want peace.

Me: Why is it so
hard to
communicate my
needs?

Higher Self:
Because then you'd
have to accept how
worthy you are of
having those needs
met.

Me: Do people like me?

Higher Self: Oh geez

Me: What?

Higher Self: Yes
people like you and
maybe some don't
but I feel like you're
just searching for
something to feel
insecure about rn.
You need to chill boo
you're good!

Me: I have the biggest crush on that person but I don't know if I'm hot or cool enough.

Higher Self: I am the divine intelligence of nature cocooned in the structural magnificence of my ancestral DNA, housing remnants of galactic stardust. That person could be a good match.

Me: The future is bleak.

Higher Self: Your attitude is bleak, stop pretending to know the future and be present with gratitude now.

Me: How can you ask me to love everyone when people are so cruel in the world?

Higher Self: Loving someone doesn't mean you condone their behavior, it means you see through it to the truth - they are suffering. Your job is to help end the needless pain their suffering is causing the world.

Me: I believe
in myself.

Higher Self:
I believe in
all of us.

Me: What does it mean to be an activist?

Higher Self: A willingness to activate the power you already have within yourself to empower others.

Me: I don't wanna work a day
job. I wanna make art full time
but I also don't wanna be
ungrateful because I have a job
and a lot of people don't.

Higher Self:
Having goals doesn't
negate your gratitude.
In fact your gratitude is an
example of your wisdom and
builds confidence to pursue
your passion. Gratitude sends
a message to the Universe
thatyou trust in its timing,
that you will respect new
opportunities and not
take them for granted
when they come your way.

Me: I want to meet the one person out there that will complete me.

Higher Self: Hi, nice to meet you!

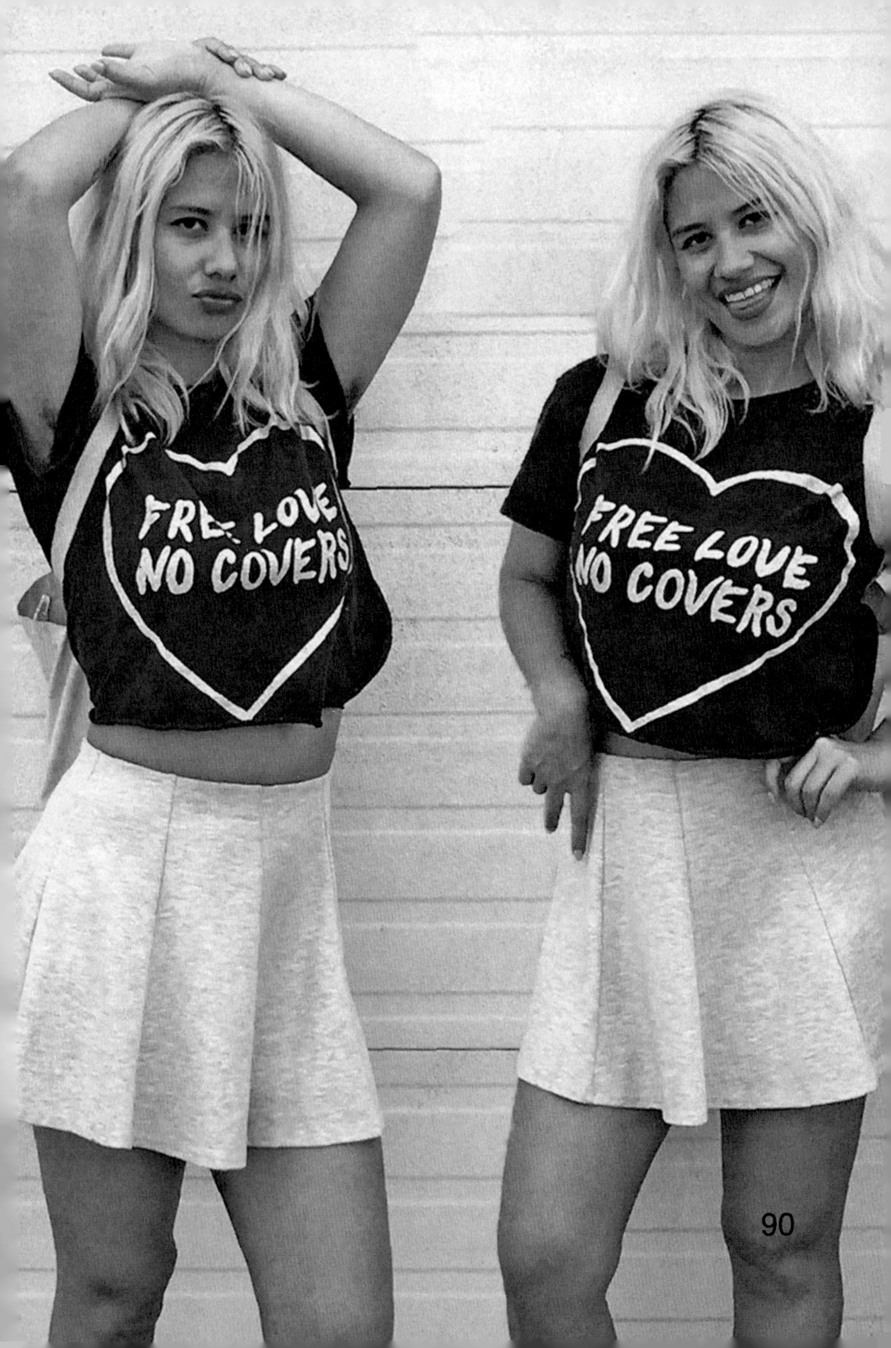

Me: I want a perfect body.

Higher Self: Forces of repression have brainwashed generations to hate the perfect beauty that is the body in all its forms. These forces have denied the awesomeness of a form so spectacular it creates life, self heals, and it the cumulative pain and pleasure of your ancestors before you.

Me:
I make art.

Higher Self:
I am art.

93

Me: How can people be so greedy when other people are suffering?

Higher Self: Greed is a form of suffering but some can't see that. They are blinded in illusion. They treat materiality as their God. Their power lies in perceiving themselves as more deserving than others. Maybe they never felt authentic love in their life, maybe their privilege has blinded them, maybe their own personal trauma turned everyone into an enemy. That is why we must heal ourselves so we don't become that. 94

Me: Why can't I always be happy?

Higher Self: What if happiness isn't what you think. What if its not these fleeting moments of validation from "good" things that happen to you? What if it is the truth inside you- simply just being you- just how you are? What if it's not temporary but always there, waiting for you to come back home?

**Me: Dear Universe,
Please let me book this
job, I really want it!**

**Higher Self:
Dear Universe,
Help me to remember
that if I don't book
this job it wasn't the
right fit. Help me
lessen my attachment
to outcomes, give me
courage to continue and
keep my heart open to
all possibilities.**

Me: Is it just me or does everyday feel like a new challenge? Like can I get a break?

Higher Self: You can give yourself a break by knowing you're doing your best and taking one day at a time because without challenges how can you grow?

97

Me: What she said hurt my feelings. Why can't she just admit she was wrong?

Higher Self. The places where people get it wrong are the places they are wounded. All of us are trying to heal and all of us make mistakes along the way.

Me: Life feels hard today.

Higher Self: When days are hard remember I'm always here whispering to you, "Soft, soft, soft... be soft with your heart today love".

Me: There are forces out there that will stop at nothing to keep people oppressed. Its scary.

Higher Self: I'd rather die fighting for love then live hiding in fear.

Me: Why do we sometimes hurt the people we love the most?

Higher Self: Relationships are our mirrors to the places we are still wounded. Sometimes we miss the opportunity to heal those places and blame the people we love for our triggers.

Me: I can do whatever I want.

Higher Self: True! But sometimes you do exactly what you don't want, thinking in the moment you do cus what feels good in the moment might not feel so good in the long run. So when you make important decisions ask me first ok? 103

Me: Gotta make that money.

Higher Self: Gotta make that money to enable me to better contribute my creative energy to help bring financial equality on this planet.

Me: Don't f*ck
with me.

Higher Self:
F*ck with me
cus I got
something
to teach you.

Me: I don't want to be alone.

Higher Self: With me, you never are because I am the Eternal Spirit inside of you that is connected to the loving consciousness of the entire Universe, where every soul beats from the same heart. There is no such thing as alone because there is only One.

Me: Everything is falling apart.

Higher Self: Good because we need to rebuild.

Me: How can I not take
things personally when
someone disrespects me?

Higher Self: What that
person said has
nothing to do with
you but everything
to do with how they
feel about themselves.
Don't forget most people
have a lot of baggage,
pain and growing to do,
just like you. Say your
peace, send them a
blessing and let's
keep it moving.

Me: I wanna be loved.

Higher Self: I love you.

Me: I wanna be accepted.

Higher Self: I accept you.

Me: I wanna be taken care of.

Higher Self: I take care of you.

Me. I know you do but what about other people?

Higher Self: Without me you can't see the love that other people have for you. Look at yourself through my eyes you'll see the truth.

110

Me: The whole country feels sick.

Higher Self:
The sickness was the illusion that everything was ok, the sickness was the lies that were shoved under the rug, the pain that didn't have a voice. Now we are taking our medicine. And its hard and it will take courage but we will never fall asleep to the sickness again.

Me: My ambition is to be successful.

Higher Self: My ambition is to remember that true success is to accept myself for who I am right in this moment.

Me: When I look at myself, I don't like what I see.

Higher Self: You were raised in a system that profits from the belief you will never be enough or have enough. Self love is a radical choice.

Me: I've been hurt so
it's really
hard for me to let
love in.

Higher Self: Love is
a state of
awareness.
You don't need
to let love "in" you
need to connect
to the love that's
already inside.

Me: I'm so in love with this person. They complete me.

Higher Self: They know their own completeness and I know mine, so when we are together our frequencies transcend to an ecstatic love dimension.

Me: Am I cool?

Higher Self: Being kind, generous, giving and knowing you're no better and no worse than any other person is what's cool. So it's really up to you.

Me: I want all my dreams to come true.

Higher Self: May the Universe use me and the gifts it has bestowed on me for the greater awakening of love on this planet. May I be of service to the whole and may the collective dream of peace be possible.

Me: I wanna learn
to love myself.

Higher Self: I'm
unlearning the
conditioning of
my past that
taught me I'm
unlovable.

Me:
I wanna
be accepted

Higher Self:
I accept
myself.

Me: Fake it til you make it.

Higher Self:
Be proud of your authentic self and watch the Universe unfold in possibility for you.

Me:
Who's
the real me?

Higher Self:
I am.

Me: I feel lost.

Higher Self: You're never lost cus you're always exactly where you need to be.

Me: I guess I never told my story cus I didn't want to be judged.

Higher Self: I think the truth is you were judging yourself love. Now you can tell your story.

Me: Don't ever leave me.

Higher Self: I never will.

Index of Hashtags